The Indian Wars

Researching American History

edited by
JoAnne Weisman Deitch

Canonicus, 1565-1647, was the leader of the Narragansetts when the Pilgrims landed in New England. He is pictured here with a gun given to him by the settlers. Historians believe there were more than 10,000 Narragansetts in 1610, but fewer than 500 remained by 1682, due to massacres, disease, and starvation. Today there are more than 2,400 members of the tribe, living primarily in Rhode Island.

Discovery Enterprises, Ltd.
Carlisle, Massachusetts

D1225722

First Edition © Discovery Enterprises, Ltd., Carlisle, MA 2000

ISBN 1-57960-087-5

Library of Congress Control Number 2002110608

10   9   8   7   6   5   4   3   2   1

Printed in the United States of America

Subject Reference Guide:

Title: *The Indian Wars*

Series*: Researching American History*

edited by JoAnne Weisman Deitch

Nonfiction

The Indian Wars, Colonial period to 1890

Credits:

Cover art: Hanyery and his people helped the Americans battle the Iroquois at Oriskany.
Art by Daniel Faulkner, South Plymouth, NY.
Found at http://oneida_nation.net/hanyery/panel 15-1.html

Other graphics are credited where they appear in the book.

Contents

About the Series

Researching American History is a series of books which introduces various topics and periods in our nation's history through the study of primary source documents.

Reading the Historical Documents

On the following pages you'll find words written by people during or soon after the time of the events. This is firsthand information about what life was like back then. Illustrations are also created to record history. These historical documents are called **primary source materials**.

At first, some things written in earlier times may seem difficult to understand. Language changes over the years, and the objects and activities described might be unfamiliar. Also, spellings were sometimes different. Below is a model which describes how we help with these challenges.

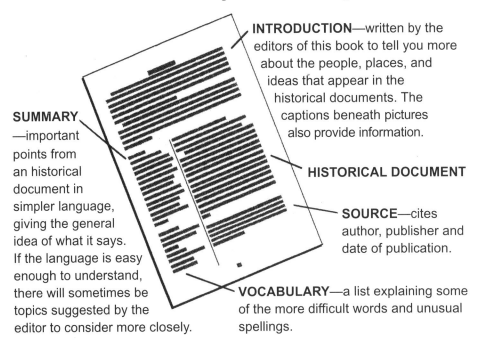

INTRODUCTION—written by the editors of this book to tell you more about the people, places, and ideas that appear in the historical documents. The captions beneath pictures also provide information.

SUMMARY—important points from an historical document in simpler language, giving the general idea of what it says. If the language is easy enough to understand, there will sometimes be topics suggested by the editor to consider more closely.

HISTORICAL DOCUMENT

SOURCE—cites author, publisher and date of publication.

VOCABULARY—a list explaining some of the more difficult words and unusual spellings.

In these historical documents, you may see three periods (…) called an ellipsis. It means that the editor has left out some words or sentences. You may see some words in brackets, such as [and]. These are words the editor has added to make the meaning clearer. When you use a document in a paper you're writing, you should include any ellipses and brackets it contains, just as you see them here. Be sure to give complete information about the author, title, and publisher of anything that was written by someone other than you.

Introduction

by
JoAnne Weisman Deitch

Ever since the first Europeans came to the area of North America which is now the United States, there have been clashes with the native peoples who had been living on this land for centuries. With the arrival of Coronado in the Southwest, to the early Eastern settlements in Jamestown and Plimoth, the people who had lived under self-rule for hundreds of years were now battered by constant invasions and conflicts. During this period of 350 years, no part of the Indian nation—from coast to coast—was spared. Conquest of the people and possession of the land became priorities for the stream of immigrants and explorers from Spain, England, France, and the Netherlands.

The conflicts between the native tribes and the Europeans also caused rifts between the tribes, as one group or another aligned itself with one or another of the warring factions. As tribes formed alliances with a European group, they hoped that their own interests would be better protected. Yet, after centuries of battles and broken promises from the white man and the newly formed government, the Native Americans were forced to give up their homelands and submit to the white man's law. However, despite their loss of control of the land, many of the tribes remain intact to this day, due to their strong cultural identities.

In this anthology, the reader will look at some of the most memorable battles from East to West and North to South. They are arranged chronologically, although many hundreds of major battles and skirmishes have been left out, due to lack of space. In our nation's early colonial history, the British, French, Dutch, and Spanish all enlisted native tribes in their battles, often fighting against other tribes who aligned themselves with opposing forces. After the War of 1812, the U.S. government moved most tribes farther and farther west to make room for white settlers. As the nation grew and expanded even further west, most of the battles which ensued were fought between U.S. military forces and the Indians, and were centered around land or mineral rights. Tribes were forced onto reservations following long and often bloody conflicts. The Battle of Wounded Knee in 1890, between the Sioux and the U.S. Cavalry, finally ended the period known as the Indian Wars.

The Colonial Period

European settlers and the Native Americans they encountered upon arriving in North America had few problems with each other, at first. When disagreements or problems arose, they were usually treated by negotiating contracts and treaties that were fair to both sides. For the most part, the Indians and settlers traded with each other, and shared peaceful coexistence. The first major war between Native Americans of the Northeast and New England's European settlers came in 1637, with the Pequot War.

The Pequot War of 1637

The colonists of Massachusetts Bay and the Pilgrim Colonies felt that they had been given the right to settle in the New World and became intolerant of the non Christian native Pequot tribe in the 1630s. Up until that time, the Pequots' only threat from an enemy had been that of the rival Narragansett tribe. When the tribe split into two factions (The Pequot and Mohegan sub-sachems) in 1631, the tribe as a whole was weakened. After a smallpox epidemic suffered by the Pequots in 1633-34 wiped out almost half of the tribe, leaving about 3,000, the Pequot nation was poised on the verge of disaster. On May 26, 1637, a military force led by John Underhill and John Mason, and supported by the Mohegan sub-sachem, attacked the Pequot village near New Haven, Connecticut and killed over 500 natives. Their leader, Sassacus, was captured on July 28th. The surviving Pequot were divided up as slaves amongst the Mohegan, Narragansett, and Eastern Niantic tribes, or became servants to New England colonists. Brief excerpts from the *Narratives of the Pequot War*, by John Mason follow.

Vocabulary:
Sachem = chief

IN the Beginning of May 1637 there were sent out by Connecticut Colony Ninety Men under the Command of Capt. John Mason against the Pequots, with Onkos [Uncas] an Indian Sachem living at Mohegan, who was newly revolted from the Pequots;...

. . . .

On the Thursday about eight of the Clock in the Morning, we Marched thence towards Pequot, with about five hundred Indians:

Vocabulary:
plunder = things looted or
  robbed during a war

…At length Onkos and one Wequash appeared; We demanded of them, Where was the Fort? They answered On the Top of that Hill: Then we demanded, Where were the Rest of the Indians? They answered, Behind, exceedingly afraid: We wished them to tell the rest of their Fellows, That they should by no means Fly, but stand at what distance they pleased, and see whether English Men would now Fight or not. Then Capt. Underhill came up, who Marched in the Rear; and commending ourselves to God, divided our Men: There being two Entrances into the Fort, intending to enter both at once: Captain Mason leading up to that on the North East Side; who approaching within one Rod, heard a Dog bark and an Indian crying Owanux! Owanux! which is Englishmen! Englishmen! We called up our Forces with all expedition, gave Fire upon them…the Indians being in a dead indeed their last Sleep:

…We had formerly concluded to destroy them by the Sword and save the Plunder.

Whereupon Captain Mason seeing no Indians, entred a Wigwam; where he was beset with many Indians, waiting.…

…The Captain also said, We must Burn them;…and stepping into the Wigwam where he had been before, brought out a Firebrand, and putting it into the Matts with which they were covered, set the Wigwams on Fire. Lieutenant Thomas Bull and Nicholas Omsted beholding, came up; and when it was thoroughly kindled, the Indians ran as Men most dreadfully Amazed.

continued on next page

7

Vocabulary:

impregnable = unable to
    be invaded or captured

Mistick = Mystic

…And when the Fort was thoroughly Fired, Command was given, that all should fall off and surround the Fort;…

The Fire was kindled on the North East Side to windward; which did swiftly over-run the Fort, to the extream Amazement of the Enemy, and great Rejoycing of our selves.

. . . .

Thus were they now at their Wits End, who not many Hours before exalted themselves in their great Pride, threatning and resolving the utter Ruin and Destruction of all the English….

…In one Hour's space was their impregnable Fort with themselves utterly Destroyed, to the Number of six or seven Hundred, as some of themselves confessed. There were only seven taken captive, and about seven escaped.

. . . .

The place of the Fort being called Mistick, this Fight was called Mistick Fight: And Mr. Increase Mather, from a Manuscript he met with, tells us; It was on Friday, May 26. 1637, a memorable Day!

The Pequots' numbers in Connecticut dwindled to 66 in the census of 1910, but has since grown to about 1000. (In 1976, they recovered their 600 acre reservation, which the state of Connecticut had sold without the tribe's permission in 1856, and are now the wealthiest tribe in America, due to their highly profitable gambling facility which opened in 1992.)

King Philip's War
1689-1697

King Philip's War was one of the most devastating of the colonial period. Although Gov. William Bradford had worked hard with Wampanoag leader Massasoit to maintain peaceful relations between the two groups in the Plymouth area, after the death of Bradford (in 1657) and Massasoit (in 1660), the colonists' greed for land and power led to unfair treatment of the natives by government leaders. When Massasoit's elder son, Wamsutta, died in 1662, his younger son, Metacom (nick-named by the English "King Philip") became the leader of the tribe. He declared to the colonists "I am determined not to live until I have no country."

Fighting began between the colonists and the Wampanoag, after Wampanoag braves killed some English-owned cattle near Bristol, Rhode Island. The natives felt that cattle were continually trampling the Indians' corn. Many natives joined with the British colonists against King Philip's warriors, and Philip was killed by a Wampanoag who was fighting with Capt. Benjamin Church's troops in 1676.

Battles were waged throughout Rhode Island, Massachusetts, New Hampshire, Connecticut, and as far north as Vermont. Thousands lost their lives on both sides. One woman, captured in an Indian raid in Lancaster, recounted her story. She was subsequently freed for ransom, when the Indians began to lose their position of power.

Account of Mary Rowlandson

"At length they came and beset our own house (which served as the garrison) and quickly it was the dolefullest day that ever mine eyes saw. The house stood upon the edge of a hill. Some of the Indians got behind the hill, others into the barn, and others behind anything that would shelter them, from all which places they shot against the house, so that the bullets seemed to fly like hail.

"Some in our house were fighting for their lives, others wallowing in their blood, the house on fire over our heads, and the bloody heathen ready to knock us on the head if we stirred out. Now might we hear mothers and children crying out for themselves and one another, 'Lord what shall we do?'"

Vocabulary:

dolefullest = most filled with grief, saddest

heathen = one who follows a tribal religion, rather than Christianity or Judaism

Source: *King Philip's War in New England (America's First Major Indian War)* by Michael Tougias. Found at www.historyplace.com/specials/king-philip.htm

The Deerfield Raid of 1704

French and Indian Raid on Deerfield, Massachusetts, February 29, 1704. Illustration from Rev. John Williams' Redeemed Captive Returning to Zion, *in which he told of his adventures as a captive. His account was a best seller throughout the colonies.*

Between 1702 and 1713, the French and British were engaged in Queen Anne's War, battling to gain control of the continent. Many native tribes sided with the French, and helped them in their attacks against the British and the colonists.

The colonists in New England demanded the French show their loyalty by staging an attack on the English. In the winter of 1704, a group of Abenakis, Caughnawagas, and French Canadians crept over high drifts of snow and surprised 290 settlers as they lay asleep in their beds in Deerfield, Massachusetts. "Thus this representative of a Christian nation, sent an army through the wilderness, not to fight an English force, but to surprise and butcher the settlers of an English plantation three hundred miles away, merely to keep on good terms with a savage tribe…. It was an act of hardly less than cold-blooded murder." (Source: John Williams, *Redeemed Captive Returning to Zion*, 1707.)

Fifty-six men, women, and children were killed, and over 100 survivors were taken captive and forced to march to Canada. Twenty-one of them died along the way. After a year of captivity, 61 of the colonists returned to Massachusetts, while others chose to remain with the Indians or their French Canadian captors.

Natives often captured colonists during the colonial period, and many, like those taken to Canada from Deerfield, chose to live the remainder of their years with the Indians. One such case, documented in a memoir written in 1824, was the story of Mary Jemison, captured by the Senecas in the 1750s, during the French and Indian War. Two brief excerpts from her dictated history follow.

Mary Jemison recalls her life with the Senecas

No people can live more happy than the Indians did in times of peace, before the introduction of spiritous liquors among them. Their lives were a continual round of pleasures. Their wants were few, and easily satisfied, and their cares were only for to-day—the bounds of their calculation for future comfort not extending to the incalculable uncertainties of to-morrow. If peace ever dwelt with men, it was in former times, in the recess from war, among what are now termed barbarians. The moral character of the Indians was (if I may be allowed the expression) uncontaminated. Their fidelity was perfect, and became proverbial. They were strictly honest; they despised deception and falsehood; and chastity was held in high veneration, and a violation of it was considered sacrilege. They were temperate in their desires, moderate in their passions, and candid and honorable in their expression.…

Source: James E. Seaver, *The Life of Mary Jemison: The White Woman of the Genesee,* 1824; 5th edition, New York, 1877.

Consider this:
Mary Jemison was clearly impressed with the honorable lifestyle of the Indians in times of peace. Think about some other situation you know of where "good people" did "bad things." Explain.

Vocabulary:
barbarians = fierce people
bounds = limits
calculation = estimate
candid = honest
chastity = purity
fidelity = loyalty
incalculable = cannot be measured
proverbial = widely referred to
temperate = moderate, self-restrained
veneration = respect

continued on next page

Artist Benjamin West portrays a captive child clinging to his Indian mother when a white man comes to take him back to his biological mother. (New York Public Library)

Consider this:

In this excerpt from Mary Jemison, she describes her adoption ceremony. Do you think it is unusual that she was adopted to "supply the place" of the brother who had been lost?

...I afterwards learned that the ceremony I at that time passed through, was that of adoption. The two squaws had lost a brother in Washington's war, sometime in the year before, and I in consequence of his death went up to Fort Pitt, on the day on which I arrived there, in order to receive a prisoner or an enemy's scalp, to supply their loss....

It was my happy lot to be accepted for adoption; and at the time of the ceremony I was received by the two squaws, to supply the place of their brother in the family; and I was ever considered and treated by them as a real sister, the same as though I had been born of their mother.

Source: Found in Peter Nabakov, ed. "Mary Jemison Becomes an Iroquois," *Native American Testimony — An Anthology of Indian and White Relations, First Encounter to Dispossession*, NY: Thomas Y. Crowell, 1978, pp. 90-5.

Tuscarora Indian War

The Indian wars of the colonial period were not fought only in New England. After years of skirmishes in the South involving Native Americans and Europeans, in 1711 war broke out in North Carolina between the British settlers and the Tuscarora. "The Indians had no concept of 'private property,' as applied to the land. Only among the Delawares was it customary for families, during certain times of the year, to be assigned specific hunting territories. Apparently this was an unusual practice, not found among other Indians. Certainly, the idea of an individual having exclusive use of a particular piece of land was completely strange to Native Americans....That is, the entire community owned the land upon which it lived..." (Source: John Alexander Williams, *West Virginia: A History for Beginners*. Found at: http://www.wvculture. org/history/indland) The English settlers, however, were not interested in sharing the land and natural resources.

On September 22, 1711, Indians staged a surprise attack on the small settlements along the Neuse and Trent Rivers in North Carolina. "At dawn on the 22nd the war whoop was heard throughout the colony," according to historian Walter Clark in his account entitled *Indian Massacre And Tuscarora War 1711-'13*. "The domesticated Indians in the homes of the whites answered the signal of those lurking in the woods, and the massacre began.... No age or sex was spared. The slaughter was indiscriminate and the wonder is any escaped. The torch was applied and those who had hidden themselves were forced out and killed.... The savages infuriated by the liquor they found commenced a systematic man hunt, and for three days the carnival of blood continued."

The Indians continued down river to New Berne, where they wiped out over one-third of the white population. "It's important that people understand the abuses endured by the Indians for a decade and the events that led up to the massacre," says East Carolina University archaeologist Dr. John E. Byrd. "Had the tables been turned, had the Indians been kidnapping colonial women and children, the colonists would have resorted to violence very quickly."

Walter Clark speculated that two of the more feasible reasons for the "bloody and remarkable outbreak of 1711" were (1) the steady encroachment upon hunting and fishing grounds that threatened their livelihood and forced them to move farther and farther from the burying grounds of their ancestors, and (2) they saw the whites engage in conflicts between themselves. This made the settlers appear divided and weakened. It encouraged the Indians to seize opportunity to remove the intruders."

The Indians resented the English building settlements on their hunting grounds and knew that the whites would eventually try to take all their lands. Hugh Talmage Lefler and Albert Ray Newsome of the University of North Carolina did extensive research on this period in American history, and found that "When the settlers purchased lands, in many cases, they failed to pay what the natives asked, as is revealed in various court records of the time." "In 1701, the Indians along the Pamlico complained to Lawson [a surveyor] that the English 'were very wicked people and that they threatened the Indians for hunting near their plantations'"

One of the greatest grievances, however, was the white practice of kidnapping Indians, particularly women and children. The practice was carried on so extensively that, according to Lefler and Newsome, the Pennsylvania legislature in 1705 passed a law against "the further importation of Indian slaves from Carolina."

Vocabulary:

pretense = a false appearance; an act of pretending

[The whites] "cheated these Indians in trading, and would not allow them to hunt near their plantations, and under that pretense took away from them their game, arms and ammunition," [and] "these poor Indians, insulted in many ways by a few rough Carolinians more barbarous and unkind than the savages themselves, could not stand such treatment much longer, and began to think of their safety and of revenge."

Source: Baron Christopher De Graffenreid, (in charge of surveying the area, and Lawson's employer.) Found in Lefler and Newsome web site www.wvculture.org/history/indland

Since Native American records of the events in North Carolina and other colonies were not written down, almost all of what we look at today has been recorded by white settlers, and show their biases. Following are some descriptions of the Tuscarora by Stanley South.

"The Indians naturally respected the whites; since they were dependent on the white people for a great many valuable articles such as guns, knives, hatchets, and other such instruments. Also after once tasting the white man's 'water of life' the weak minded Indian would do almost anything for another mouthful of it. The white people thus assumed a position of superiority over the Indians without objection on their part."

[By the year 1711, the settlers] "were now treading upon the heels of a tribe or family of tribes as warlike, cruel, and cunning as any in the United States. Their numbers were considerable also. They could muster 1200 or 1500 fighting men. They inhabited a great section of territory bordering and north of the Neuse River. They were directly in the path of the advancing settlers and were not of a nature to be encroached upon or to surrender their lands without a struggle."

"The Indians lived an unsystematic, intemperate and unsanitary sort of life," South wrote. "They took little care of themselves, keeping well by virtue of much healthful, strenuous, outdoor exercise. They had some valuable knowledge of medicinal herbs and of healing wounds; but with all this their medical ability was very crude and limited. They lived by keeping well rather than by any ability to make a sick person well again…. It is said that taken with it (smallpox) they would frequently rush into a stream and drown themselves through hopeless despair."

continued on next page

Consider this:
Today, doctors recommend that people practice preventive medicine, using exercise and good eating habits. Was this what the Indians practiced? Explain your answer.

Things to do:
Make a list of the points made by the author that seem biased, rather than objective.

Vocabulary:
encroached = trespassed
intemperate = indulgent, not moderate
'water of life' = alcoholic beverages, liquor

15

Things to do:
List the reasons South gives for the demise of the Indian.

Vocabulary:
debased = degraded, lowered
degenerated = deteriorated
demise = death
diminshed = decreased
harassed = annoyed

[South said rum was a very important influence in the demise of the North Carolina Tuscarora]: "This evil was introduced among them by the first white people with whom they came in contact, for it was inseparable from the adventurers of those times…. Once having tasted it, a craving for it which the weak-willed Indians could not withstand seized them. They called it firewater and the more it burned them the more they desired it…. Great numbers debased and shortened their lives.

"Furthermore, the race degenerated in other ways from their contact with the whites," South continued. "By it the Indians became unable to pursue their former strenuous life….

"They weakened their bodies and corrupted that which they possessed of intelligence. They were unceasingly harassed by the whites and frequently forced to change their hunting grounds…the Indian population diminished by war, disease, effect of rum, failure to reproduce themselves rapidly due to degeneration of the race, melted away on coming in contact with the white settlers."

Source: Found at www.ncsu.edu/stud_orgs/native_american/nctribes_orgs/ncnahistory.html

Eighteenth Century Indian Wars

The struggle for dominance in the New World between Britain and France continued to pit Indian tribes against each other as they aligned themselves with one side or the other of the European forces. By the 1750s, the fighting had spread beyond the Appalachian Mountains to the Great Lakes. Although the French had many advantages in the French and Indian War (1754-1763), England finally prevailed. In 1763, with the outbreak of Pontiac's rebellion in the Great Lakes Region, Ottawa and other tribes stormed Detroit, and the rebellion of Pontiac collapsed. From that time on, white settlement beyond the Appalachian Mountains was not permitted by the English.

The French and Indian War

Sir William Johnson and the Indians
by Mary Alice Burke Robinson

One of the great historical figures to emerge in the French and Indian War is Sir William Johnson of the Mohawk Valley in New York. Sir William was commissioned by King George II in 1753 to obtain the support of the Iroquois on the side of the British. He was successful in this because he was respected and trusted by the Indians.

In 1756, he was made "Superintendent of Indian Affairs for the Northern District" and received a commission as "Colonel of the Six Nations" (the Iroquois). He led militia and Indians into battle on more than one occasion and was totally committed to Indian affairs, often traveling long distances to meet at council fires.

French officers were aware of the relationship between Johnson and the Iroquois as Louis de Bougainville stated over and over in his journals. Bougainville was aide-de-camp to Marquis de Montcalm during the French and Indian War and kept a journal throughout his stay in America. An excerpt follows.

"Johnson concerns himself only with Indian affairs, he is the chief of that department. He has gathered together four or five hundred Indians from the regions of the Delaware, the Susquehanna, Seneca, etc., that we call Moraigans

continued on next page

[Mohicans]. We do not know the destination of the Mohawks, to the number of one hundred, who have taken up the hatchet against us."

"Johnson has gone off again with all his Indians; a body of three thousand men and five six-pounders have followed him toward the Mohawk River."

Source: Bougainville, Louis Antoine de, comte, *Adventure in the Wilderness; the American Journals of Louis Antoine de Bougainville*, translated and edited by Edward P. Hamilton, 1st ed., Norman, University of Oklahoma, 1964, pp. 35, 246.

Sir William Johnson was a devoted and loyal champion of the Indians. He was willing to persist in matters where they needed a prominent and respected person to represent them. Much of his time was spent attending to Indian affairs as his manuscripts show, meeting with the Indians, listening to their demands as they bargained with one another, trading wampum belts, and goods and supplies for warriors. He was accessible to them and maintained an almost paternalistic attitude toward the Indians who needed constant reassurance accompanied by tangible proof of promises made to them. They, in turn, trusted and respected him.

1760 April 8 Fort Johnson - Sir William Johnson to Brig. Gen Gage, asking permission to feed Mohawks impoverished by destruction of their crops by droves of cattle passing through their fields, presenting their claim for damages, and asking for wagons and boats.

1760 April 13 Albany - Thomas Gage, consenting to furnish wagons and boats; promising to order provisions to be issued to Mohawks at Forts Hunter and Hendrick and to refer claim to Gen Amherst...

1760 April 25 Fort Johnson - Sir William Johnson to Gen Gage, pressing the matter of boats and wagons to carry Indian stores, denouncing deputy quartermasters who withhold them...

Source: Richard E. Day, Compiler, *Calendar of the Sir William Johnson Manuscripts* in the New York State Library, Albany, University of the State of New York, 1909, pp. 102-175.

Pontiac's Conspiracy

Pontiac's Rebellion (Ohio Historical Society)

Pontiac, the chief of the Ottawa, united tribes in the Great Lakes region and in the Ohio and Mississippi river valleys in the hopes of driving settlers out of the area. During the French and Indian War (1754-1763), Pontiac began a two-year siege, known as Pontiac's War, against British garrisons in the region, which ended in his surrender in 1765.

Pontiac secretly organized a general uprising which caught the British totally by surprise. After it began in May of 1763, the rebellion captured nine of the twelve British forts west of the Appalachians. However, an informer warned the garrison, and Pontiac failed in the critical mission he had reserved for himself–taking Fort Detroit. The Delaware, Shawnee, and Mingo surrounded Fort Pitt cutting if off from the outside world and then attacked the Pennsylvania frontier killing 600 colonists. In an effort to break the siege at Fort Pitt, Amherst wrote its commander, Captain Simeon Ecuyer, suggesting that he deliberately infect the tribes outside the fort by giving them blankets and handkerchiefs infected with smallpox. Ecuyer did exactly this, and the resulting epidemic spread from the Delaware, Shawnee, and Mingo to the Cherokee in Tennessee and then the entire Southeast. (Source: Found at http://www.tolatsga.org/dela.html)

Pontiac Makes an Alliance

My brothers, we have never had in view to do you any evil. We have never intended that any should be done you. But amongst my young men there are, as amongst you, some who, in spite of all precautions which we take, always do evil. Besides, it is not only for my revenge

continued on next page

19

Things to do:
Summarize Pontiac's message to his fellow Indians.

Vocabulary:
annihilation = utter destruction
avenging = taking revenge

Source: Wayne Moquin, editor, *Great Documents in American Indian History,* New York: Praeger Publishers. 1973, pp. 124-5. Found in Karen Luisa Badt, *Indians of the Northeast,* Perspectives on History Series, Discovery Enterprises, Ltd., Carlisle, MA 1997, pp. 41-3.

that I make war upon the English, it is for you my brothers, as for us. When the English, in their councils, which we have held with them, have insulted us, they have also insulted you, without your knowing anything about it, and as I know all our brothers know, the English have taken from you all means of avenging yourselves, by disarming you and making you write on a paper, which they have sent to their country, which they could not make us do; therefore, I will avenge you equally with us, and I swear their annihilation as long as any of them shall remain on our land.... I am the same French Pondiak who lent you his hand seventeen years ago. I am a Frenchman, and I want to die a Frenchman! And I repeat to you they are both your interests and mine which I revenge. Let me go on. I don't ask your assistance, because I know you cannot give it. I only ask of you Provisions for me and all my people. If, however, you would like to aid me, I would not refuse you. You would cause me pleasure, and you would the sooner be out of trouble. For I warrant you, when the English shall be driven from here or killed, we shall all retire to our villages according to our custom, and await the arrival of our father, the Frenchman. These, you see, my brothers, are my sentiments. Rest assured, my brothers, I will watch that no more wrong shall be done to you by my people, nor by other Indians. What I ask of you is that our women be allowed to plant our corn on the fallows [clearings] of your lands. We shall be obliged to you for that.

When the French and Indian War was officially over in 1763, the colonies of North America were only 13 years away from the Revolutionary War. Peaceful coexistence was not on the agenda, and the Indian Wars amongst the natives, the white colonists and European settlers escalated.

Royal Proclamation of 1763

On October 7, King George III signed the Royal Proclamation of 1763 establishing that most of the land gained from the French in the recently concluded French and Indian War was closed to white settlers.

...whereas it is just and reasonable, and essential to our Interest, and the Security of our Colonies, that the several Nations or Tribes of Indians with whom We are connected, and who live under our Protection, should not be molested or disturbed in the Possession of such Parts of Our Dominions and Territories as, not having been ceded to or purchased by Us, are reserved to them, or any of them, as their Hunting Grounds—We do therefore…declare it to be our Royal Will and Pleasure, that no Governor or Commander in Chief in any of our Colonies of Quebec, East Florida, or West Florida, do presume, upon any Pretence whatever, to grant Warrants of Survey, or pass any Patents for Lands beyond the Bounds of their respective Governments, as described in their Commissions: as also that no Governor or Commander in Chief in any of our other Colonies or Plantations in America do presume for the present, and until our further Pleasure be known, to grant Warrants of Survey, or pass Patents for any Lands beyond the Heads or Sources of any of the Rivers which fall into the Atlantic Ocean from the West and North West, or upon any Lands whatever, which, not having been ceded to or purchased by Us as aforesaid, are reserved to the…Indians, or any of them. And We do further declare it to be Our Royal Will and Pleasure, for the present as aforesaid, to reserve under our Sovereignty, Protection, and Dominion, for the use of the said Indians, all the Lands and

Vocabulary:
ceded = surrendered
Dominion = realm, domain
Pretence = a false show
Sovereignty = authority, power

continued on next page

Territories not included within the Limits of Our said Three new Governments, or within the Limits of the Territory granted to the Hudson's Bay Company, as also all the Lands and Territories lying to the Westward of the Sources of the Rivers which fall into the Sea from the West and North West as aforesaid....

And We do hereby strictly forbid, on Pain of our Displeasure, all our loving Subjects from making any Purchases or Settlements whatever, or taking Possession of any of the Lands above reserved, without our especial leave and Licence for that Purpose first obtained....

And We do further strictly enjoin and require all Persons whatever who have either wilfully or inadvertently seated themselves upon any Lands within the Countries above described or upon any other Lands which, not having been ceded to or purchased by Us, are still reserved to the said Indians as aforesaid, forthwith to remove themselves from such Settlements.... And whereas great Frauds and Abuses have been committed in purchasing Lands of the Indians, to the great Prejudice of our Interests, and to the great Dissatisfaction of the said Indians: In order, therefore, to prevent such Irregularities for the future, and to the end that the Indians may be convinced of our Justice and determined Resolution to remove all reasonable Cause of Discontent, We do,...require, that no private Person...make any purchase from the said Indians of any Lands reserved to the said Indians, within those parts of our Colonies where We have thought proper to allow Settlement.... And we do,...declare and enjoin, that the Trade with the said Indians shall be free and open to all our Subjects whatever, provided that every Person who may incline to Trade with the

Vocabulary:
enjoin = command
inadvertently = accidentally

22

said Indians do take out a Licence for carrying on such Trade from the Governor or Commander in Chief of any of our Colonies....

...And we do further expressly conjoin and require all Officers...to seize and apprehend all Persons whatever, who standing charged with Treason, Misprisions of Treason, Murders, or other Felonies or Misdemeanors, shall fly from Justice and take Refuge in the said Territory, and to send them under a proper guard to the Colony where the Crime was committed,...in order to take their Trial for the same.

Given at our Court at St. James's the 7th Day of October 1763, in the Third Year of our Reign.

GOD SAVE THE KING

Consider this:
The language in this document is very formal and repetitive. In the next section of this book is an article on the Indians' method of recording a contract—the wampum belt. Compare the two documents.

Vocabulary:
apprehend = arrest
conjoin = join together

Two Row Wampum – The Indians' Treaty

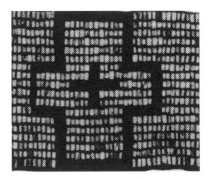

Cayuga Chief Jacob Thomas holding a replica of the Two Row Wampum.

Detail of Delaware Wampum Belt (Museum of the American Indian)

The Two Row Wampum laid the foundation for all treaties and agreements...made with Europeans during the colonial history of North America. Wampum belts were used during this period to record...events and agreements.... The Two Row embodies the principles of sharing, mutual recognition, respect and partnership and is based on a nation to nation relationship which respects the autonomy, authority and jurisdiction of each nation. The Two Row Wampum Belt symbolizes the relationship of the native people of North America,...with the Whiteman... One purple row of beads represents the path of the natives' canoe which contains their customs and laws. The other row represents the path of the Whiteman's vessel, the sailing ship, which contains his customs and laws. The meaning of the parallel paths is that neither boat should out pace the other, and the paths should remain separate and parallel forever, that is, as long as the grass grows, the rivers flow, the sun shines, and will be everlasting, and they shall always renew their treaties. (Source: Found at http://www.kahnawake.com)

Source: Excerpted from presentations to the Special Committee on Indian Self Government by the Haudenosaunee Confederacy and from Wampum Belts by Tehanetorens.

"When the Haudenosaunee first came into contact with the European Nations, treaties of peace and friendship were made. Each was symbolized by the Gus-Wen-Tah or Two Row Wampum. There is a bed of white wampum which symbolized the purity of the agreement. There are two rows of purple, and those rows have the spirit of your ancestors and mine. There are three beads of wampum separating the two rows and they symbolize peace, friendship and respect..."

Native Americans in the Revolutionary War

Battle of Oriskany on August 6, 1777

The Battle of Oriskany serves as an example of how the Revolutionary War pitted two Indian leaders against each other: Hanyery of the pro-American Oneidas, whose territory bordered the limits of white settlement, and Joseph Brant of the pro-British Mohawks living in the Mohawk Valley.

"In the late war with the people on the other side of the great water and at a period when thick darkness overspread this country, your brothers the Oneidas stepped forth, and un-invited took up the hatchet in your defense. We fought by your side, our blood flowed together, and the bones of our warriors mingled with yours."

Source: Found at http://oneida_nation.net/oriskany.html from Hough 1861 1:124.

When the Revolutionary War erupted, the Oneidas held different views about the conflict than the rest of the Iroquois Confederacy. After hundreds of years of peace and power, the Iroquois Confederacy was split by the issue of whether to side with the colonists or the British. The Oneidas made the difficult decision to remain true to their new American neighbors, believing in principle that taxation without representation and domination by the King of England was intolerable and wrong. The decision to support the colonists pitted Indian brother against Indian brother as the remaining four members of the original Iroquois Confederacy decided to remain neutral or sided with the British. (Source: Found at http://oneida_nation.net/oriskany.html)

During the campaign of 1777, in what is now the Albany area of New York, the British thought they could win the war by isolating New England from the other American colonies. Part of the British plan included securing Fort Stanwix and the Mohawk Valley. As British forces approached the Fort, Paulus, a teenage boy of Oriska, and Joseph Brant, a pro-British Mohawk, were said to have crossed paths, and had the following conversation, retold over the years in Oneida tradition. (Source: Found at http://oneida_nation.net/oriskany.html from Draper 11:204B-205.)

annihilated = wiped out,
    destroyed
bade = past tense of bid
blandishments = flattery
deplore = dislike
insinuatingly = using hints
persevere = persist
pickets = soldiers
    positioned to give
    warning of an enemy
    approach

Paulus meets Joseph Brant

Some Oneidas were inside the fort; the others outside as pickets and spies. When [Paulus] was alone & in the woods some miles in advance of the fort, he discovered the enemy approaching in the distance—& they discovered him at the same time.

Brant hailed him—begged him to stop as he was in the act retreating, pledging his honor that he should neither be hurt nor detained. So Paulus raised his gun & invited Brant to approach alone for an interview—as they then would be on an equality. But he ordered Brant as he neared him to halt a few steps off—still presenting his gun, with his finger on the trigger —and bade Brant deliver whatever message he had to offer.

Brant insinuatingly offered him a large reward & aplenty as long as he should live, if he would only join the King's side & induce other Oneidas to do so, & help the British to take Fort Stanwix. Paulus firmly rejected any such blandishments, saying he and his brother Oneidas had joined their fortunes with those of the Americans, & would share with them what-ever good or ill might come. Brant portrayed the great & resistless power of the King, and professed to deplore the ruin of the Oneidas if they should foolishly and recklessly persist in their determination. Paulus replied that he & the Oneidas would persevere, if need be, till all were annihilated; and that was all he had to say when each retired his own way.

As Paulus hastened to the fort & reached his fellow Oneida pickets, the enemy had run with equal speed, and had commenced firing on the opposite side of the fort while Paulus and his companions were entering on the other

Joseph Brandt
(Ohio Historical Society)

—& had even to fight theirin [therein]. The British then began to dig to undermine the fort, to blow it up. Oneidas used to say, if they had not been there to aid in its defense, the fort might not have been saved.

Source: Found at http://oneida_nation.net/hanyery/panel 13-1.html

...Oneidas rushed east to Saratoga where they served with distinction in the campaign ending in another British defeat. American victories in 1777 prompted France and other European nations to join the war against Great Britain. France's aid proved to be decisive in the winning of American independence.

The events of 1777, therefore, were crucial to the outcome of the Revolutionary War. In that year of destiny, the Oneida Nation contributed more to the birth of the United States than any other community of comparable size in the colonies.... (Source: Found at http://oneida_nation.net/oriskany.html)

Nineteenth Century Indian Wars

The War of 1812
by Mary Alice Burke Robinson

Britain wanted to contain the young United States within boundaries established at the end of the American Revolution. Her government proposed creating an independent state for American Indians along the U.S.-Canadian border, which would serve as a buffer zone and a deterrent to any American attempt to invade and overpower Canada. For this reason, most Indian tribes sided with Britain.

Some natives recognized that if they did not resist, they would lose all their land. They also realized that their own inter-tribal warfare had to be set aside while they faced a common enemy. Two leaders of this movement were the Shawnee, Tenskwatawa, called The Prophet, and his elder brother Tecumseh. They worked to form an Indian federation that would be powerful enough to halt white encroachment on Indian lands.

Tecumseh explained his philosophy in a speech addressed to William Henry Harrison in August of 1810.

Consider this:

How did the Indians claim the land for occupancy?

Was it a good idea to share hunting and travelling rights? Explain.

Source: Tecumseh, August 12, 1810, in Samuel G. Drake, *Biography and History of the Indians of North America*, II th ed., Boston,1841, pp. 617-8.

Tecumseh's Speech

The white people have no right to take the land from the Indians, because they had it first; it is theirs. They may sell, but all must join. Any sale not made by all is not valid. The late sale is bad. It was made by a part only. Part do not know how to sell. It requires all to make a bargain for all. All red men have equal rights to the un-occupied land. The right of occupancy is as good in one place as in another. There cannot be two occupations in the same place. The first excludes all others. It is not so in hunting or travelling; for there the same ground will serve many, as they may follow each other all day; but the camp is stationary, and that is occupancy. It belongs to the first who sits down on his blanket or skins, which he has thrown upon the ground, and till he leaves it no other has a right.

Some Indian tribes felt that Tecumseh should not encourage Indians to join with the British in their struggles against the United States. When

Tecumseh went south in 1811 to gain Indian support against the Americans in the Northeast, Choctaw Chief Pushmataha opposed Tecumseh's plan.

Chief Pushmataha's View

The war, which you are now contemplating against the Americans... forebodes nothing but destruction to our entire race. It is a war against a people whose territories are now far greater than our own, and who are far better provided with all the necessary implements of war, with men, guns, horses, wealth, far beyond that of all our race combined, and where is the necessity or wisdom to make war upon such a people?

Source: H. B. Cushman, *History of the Choctaw, Chickasaw, and Natchez Indians,* Greenville, Texas, 1899, pp. 315-8.

Vocabulary:

contemplating = thinking about, considering

Battle of Tippecanoe

In November 1811, at Tippecanoe Creek, William Henry Harrison attacked a stronghold of The Prophet, Tecumseh's brother, laying waste to the buildings and winter stores. Retaliation would come in Spring.

War is declared!

Be it enacted by the Senate and House of Representatives of the United States of America in Congress assembled, That war be and the same is hereby declared to exist between the United Kingdom of Great Britain and Ireland and the dependencies thereof, and the United States of America and their territories; and that the President of the United States is hereby authorized to use the whole land and naval force of the United States to carry the same into effect, and to issue to private armed vessels of the United States commissions or letters of marque and general reprisal, in such form as he shall think proper, and under the seal of the United States, against the vessels, goods, and effects of the government of the said United Kingdom of Great Britain and Ireland, and the subjects thereof. APPROVED, June 18, 1812

Vocabulary:

general reprisal = forcible seizure of an enemy's goods

letters of marque = documents issued by a nation allowing a citizen to seize goods or people of another nation

The Creek War
1813-1814

An Indian uprising in the South brought on the Creek Indian War (1813-1814). Creeks who lived mainly in Alabama and Georgia were alarmed by encroachments on their lands and were convinced by Tecumseh, the Shawnee chief, to unite with many other tribes against the settlers. The leader of the Creeks was William Weatherford, also known as Red Eagle. On August 30, 1813, he led an attack on Fort Mims, a temporary stockade near the confluence of the Tombigbee and Alabama rivers. Although Weatherford attempted to restrain his warriors, they massacred some 500 whites. The U.S. retaliated on November 3 when General John Coffee attacked and destroyed the Indian village Talladega, in Alabama, killing more than 500 warriors. In January 1814, however, Tennessee militiamen were defeated in three minor engagements. The war did not end until the Battle of Horseshoe Bend in March 1814.

The war ended as General Andrew Jackson defeated the Creeks under Chief Weatherford at the decisive battle of Horseshoe Bend, Alabama, where nearly 900 of 1000 Indians were killed. (Source: Gorton Carruth, "The Encyclopedia of American Facts and Dates." 10th ed., New York: Harper Collins Publishers. ©1997.)

The Massacre at Fort Mims

Indian Removal

Following the War of 1812 the United States adopted a policy of the wholesale removal of Native American peoples to the Indian Territory west of the Mississippi River. Removal was made a basic tenet of most treaties, and the first major removal treaty was signed by the Delaware in 1818. In the Southeast, the Choctaw and Creek signed removal treaties in 1820 and 1821, respectively. By 1830, President Andrew Jackson got the Indian Removal Act through Congress; this authorized the President to set up districts within the Western Indian Territory for Eastern peoples who agreed to relocate. …Entire tribes were forced to resettle, and several wars resulted when Native Americans refused to accept resettlement.

However, by 1850 the period of Indian removal was for the most part over, with only scattered groups of Native Americans remaining east of the Mississippi. West of the Mississippi River the federal government organized a reservation system to separate Native Americans from white settlers. (Source: http://www.fas.org/man/dod-101/ops/indian_wars.htm)

Andrew Jackson's View of the Indians

"Our conduct toward these people is deeply interesting to our national character. Their present condition, contrasted with what they once were, makes a most powerful appeal to our sympathies. Our ancestors found them the uncontrolled possessors of these vast regions. By persuasion and force they have been made to retire from river to river and from mountain to mountain, until some of the tribes have become extinct and others have left but remnants to preserve for awhile their once terrible names. Surrounded by the whites with their arts of civilization, which by destroying the resources of the savage doom him to weakness and decay, the fate of the Mohegan, the Narragansett, and the Delaware is fast overtaking the Choctaw, the Cherokee, and the Creek. That this fate surely awaits them if they remain within the limits of the states does not admit of a doubt. Humanity and national honor demand that every effort should be made to avert so great a calamity."

Summary:

Our conduct toward the Native Americans is interesting. We are sympathetic to them, as they were once in control of this vast land, and now they have so little. Some tribes no longer exist. The fate of other tribes is dismal. We should make an effort to support them, because of our national honor.

Consider this:

Did Jackson honor our country by how he treated the Indians?

The Indian Removal Act of 1830

The Indian Removal Act provided for an exchange of lands with Indians residing in any of the states or territories, and their removal west of the Mississippi.

Summary:

Congress enacts that it is lawful for the U.S. president to move Indians to land west of the Mississippi River and divide that land into districts in which the tribes will live.

Things to do:

Continue with the brief excerpts from sections 3 to 5, and summarize the text in your own words. Note in Section 4 that the Indians cannot claim any added value that is found on the land. (What if gold were discovered?)

Vocabulary:

revert = be returned to
subsistence = livelihood

Be it enacted by the Senate and House of Representatives of the United States of America, in Congress assembled, That it shall and may be lawful for the President of the United States to cause so much of any territory belonging to the United States, west of the river Mississippi, not included in any state or organized territory, and to which the Indian title has been extinguished, as he may judge necessary, to be divided into a suitable number of districts, for the reception of such tribes or nations of Indians as may choose to exchange the lands where they now reside, and remove there;...

SEC. 3. ..., that the United States will forever secure and guaranty to them, and their heirs or successors, the country so exchanged with them; ...Provided always, That such lands shall revert to the United States, if the Indians become extinct, or abandon the same.

SEC. 4. ...That if, upon any of the lands now occupied by the Indians,...there should be such improvements as add value to the land claimed ...it shall and may be lawful for the President to cause such value to...be paid to the person or persons rightfully claiming such improvements. And...the improvements...shall pass to the United States, and...not afterwards...to any of the same tribe.

SEC. 5. ...That...it shall and may be lawful for the President to...give them such aid and assistance as may be necessary for their support and subsistence for the first year after their removal.

The Cherokee Trail of Tears

In one of the saddest episodes of our brief history, men, women, and children were taken from their land, herded into makeshift forts with minimal facilities and food, then forced to march a thousand miles (Some made part of the trip by boat in equally horrible conditions). Under the generally indifferent army commanders, human losses for the first groups of Cherokee removed were extremely high. John Ross made an urgent appeal to Scott, requesting that the general let his people lead the tribe west. General Scott agreed. Ross organized the Cherokee into smaller groups and let them move separately through the wilderness so they could forage for food. Although the parties under Ross left in early fall and arrived in Oklahoma during the brutal winter of 1838-39, he significantly reduced the loss of life among his people. About 4000 Cherokee died as a result of the removal. The route they traversed and the journey itself became known as "The Trail of Tears" or, as a direct translation from Cherokee, "The Trail Where They Cried" (*"Nunna daul Tsuny"*). (Source:http://americanhistory.about.com/gi/dynamic offsite.)

Painting by Robert Lindneux, 1942. Woolaroc Museum

33

The Neverending Trail
by Abe "Del" Jones

We whites honor the "Hermitage"
And the man who once lived there –
But, that leader of our Nation
Was cruel, unjust, unfair –

He ordered the removal
Of the Cherokee from their land
And forced them on a trek
That the Devil must have planned –

One thousand miles of misery –
Of pain and suffering –
Because greed of the white man
Could not even wait till spring –

We should bow our heads in shame
Even unto this day
About "The Trail Of Tears"
And those who died along the way.

It was October, eighteen thirty-eight
When seven thousand troops in blue
Began the story of the "Trail"
Which, so sadly, is so true –

Jackson ordered General Scott
To rout the Indian from their home –
The "Center Of The World" they loved –
The only one they'd known –

The Braves working in the fields
Arrested, placed in a stockade –
Women and children dragged from home
In the bluecoats shameful raid –

Some were prodded with bayonets
When, they were deemed to move too slow
To where the Sky was their blanket
And the cold Earth, their pillow –

In one home a Babe had died
Sometime in the night before –
And women mourning, planning burial
Were cruelly herded out the door –

In another, a frail Mother –
Papoose on back and two in tow
Was told she must leave her home
Was told that she must go –

She uttered a quiet prayer –
Told the old family dog good-bye –
Then, her broken heart gave out
And she sank slowly down to die –

Chief Junaluska witnessed this –
Tears streaming down his face –
Said if he could have known this
It would have never taken place –

For, at the battle of Horse Shoe
With five hundred Warriors, his best –
Helped Andrew Jackson win that battle
And lay thirty-three Braves to rest –

And the Chief drove his tomahawk
Through a Creek Warrior's head
Who was about to kill Jackson –
But whose life was saved, instead –

Chief John Ross knew this story
And once sent Junaluska to plead –
Thinking Jackson would listen to
This Chief who did that deed –

But, Jackson was cold, indifferent
To the one he owed his life to
Said, "The Cherokee's fate is sealed –
There's nothing, I can do."

Washington, D.C. had decreed
They must be moved Westward –
And all their pleas and protests
To this day still go unheard.

On November, the seventeenth
Old Man Winter reared his head –
And freezing cold, sleet and snow
Littered that trail with the dead.

On one night, at least twenty-two
Were released from their torment
To join that Great Spirit in the Sky
Where all good souls are sent –

Many humane, heroic stories
Were written 'long the way –
A monument, for one of them –
Still stands until this day –

It seems one noble woman
It was Chief Ross' wife –
Gave her blanket to a sick child
And in so doing, gave her life –

She is buried in an unmarked grave –
Dug shallow near the "Trail" –
Just one more tragic ending
In this tragic, shameful tale –

Mother Nature showed no mercy
Till they reached the end of the line
When that fateful journey ended
On March twenty-sixth, eighteen thirty-nine.

Each mile of this infamous "Trail"
Marks the graves of four who died –
Four thousand poor souls in all
Marks the shame we try to hide –

You still can hear them crying
Along *The Trail Of Tears*
If you listen with your heart
And not with just your ears.

Source: Del "Abe" Jones, *The Neverending Trail,* appears
in his book, *"The World, War, Freedom, and More."*
Poem found at http://www.ngeorgia.com/history/
nghisttt.html

Consider this:
History can be recorded
in many ways: through
news accounts, journals,
paintings, photographs,
and more. In this instance,
poet Abe Jones retells the
story of the Trail of Tears
in his poem, "The Never-
ending Trail".

What has he captured
here that may not have
been expressed in prose?

Is this poem as accurate
as an eyewitness account
might have been?

What does the poet think
of Andrew Jackson?

What does "listening with
your heart" mean?

Vocabulary:
indifferent = not caring
The Hermitage = The home
    of Andrew Jackson
torment = agony

The U.S. Cavalry

General Custer's Black Hills Expedition in 1874 – 7th Cavalry Regiment. The regiment escorted prospectors searching for gold into the Black Hills of South Dakota (sacred Native American burial grounds). The influx of gold-seekers contributed to the 1876 escalation of hostilities between the Indians and government troops. Custer is in the light clothing on a horse, just left of center. (William H. Illingworth)

As the nation expanded westward, the Army Department determined that more units were needed to protect settlers and fortune seekers heading west.

Almost immediately following its activation, the Seventh Cavalry Regiment patrolled the Kansas plains for raiding Native Americans and to protect the westward movement of pioneers. From 1866 to 1881, the regiment marched a total of 181,692 miles across Kansas, Montana, and the Dakota Territories. Coupled with low pay, alcoholism, poor subsistence, and generally poor conditions, the regiment suffered ten suicides and 160 desertions....

. . . .

In 1875, the regiment also escorted a railroad survey of the Yellowstone River valley. This expedition brought the regiment into constant conflict with Native American raiding parties.... Typically, the federal government had broken every treaty it had made with the Indians. Food, supplies, and weapons that had been promised to Native Americans were instead sold for gold to the settlers. The government promised these goods to the Native Americans if the latter would peacefully remain on reserved lands. Flour and grain sent to the agencies were often mixed with sand; meat was often unfit for human consumption. Given the Native Americans' traditionally nomadic lifestyle and the poor living conditions, it was no surprise that they migrated. (Source: Found at http://www.army.mil/)

Following are several excerpts from the "History of the 1st U. S. Cavalry," found at the U.S. Military Center for History.

THE FIRST REGIMENT OF CAVALRY.
By CAPT. R. P. PAGE WAINWRIGHT,
1ST U. S. CAVALRY.

In October, 1837, and again in March, 1838, serious difficulties were reported between the settlers and the Osage Indians, and companies of the regiment were at once sent to the disturbed regions. On the second occasion the rapidity of Colonel Kearny's movements and the sudden appearance of 200 dragoons in their midst appear to have had a very quieting effect on the Indians, for after his return to Leavenworth Colonel Kearny reports no further danger of trouble with the Osages.

In April, 1839, the post of Fort Wayne, on the northwestern frontier of Arkansas, was established for the purpose of keeping the Cherokees in subjection, and by the end of October Companies E, F, G and K, were stationed there. In this same month Colonel Kearny, with Companies A, B, C, H and I, scouting, visited the post, but in November returned to Fort Leavenworth having marched about 550 miles.

. . . .

In the month of August, 1857, the regiment started on its march overland for Utah. The route was long and weary..., but when the early snows fell upon them at South Pass and the mercury went down into the bulb of the thermometer to keep from freezing, and the starved horses laid down to die on the trail, the lighthearted Dragoon,...began to think there might be some credit in being jolly. Jolly he was not always, but the survivors of that terrible winter all testify to the invariable cheerfulness and

Consider this:
How does the author describe the cold?

Did acting "jolly" help the men get through the journey to Utah?

Vocabulary:
dragoons = heavily armed troopers
subjection = brought under control

continued on next page

Consider this:

The Cavalry in the 1860s was responsible for scouting, defense, building forts, and more. Does the U.S. Army do all of that today? Report on your findings.

pluck of the soldiers; on foot, half starved and more than half frozen, they struggled on as far as Fort Bridger, and, there, passed a winter of suffering.

From this time until the year 1861 scoutings and skirmishes with the Indians were almost incessant, and portions of the regiment were always found where the fighting was going on.

Within a month after reaching Leavenworth, November, 1865, we find troops marching for the (then) frontier posts of Riley, Kearny, Hays, Lyon, Harker, Dodge, Larned and Wallace. They found the winter of 1865 and '66 one of hard work, not so much as soldiers, as mechanics and laborers, for at several of their new stations it was necessary to construct huts to protect themselves from the severity of the winter. This work was continued into the following summer, except when interrupted by scouting between the Smoky Hill and Arkansas rivers. Having succeeded in making themselves fairly comfortable, the regiment was ordered in September to march across the country, and report to its old colonel, then General, Philip St. George Cooke, commanding the Department of the Platte.

The several troops were scattered about at Forts Laramie, McPherson, Phil. Kearny, Casper, Sand and Sedgwick, and from these stations maintained an almost constant warfare with the Indians.

On December 9, 1866, Lieutenant Bingham, commanding Troop C, met his death in a skirmish near Phil. Kearny, and twelve days later 27 men of the same troop, with 3 officers and 49 men of the 18th Infantry, were killed in what is known as the "Phil. Kearny Massacre." Had the Indians received the chastisement they deserved for this bloody deed, it would have been in the end a kindness. Going unavenged, it only created in the minds of the Sioux a false idea of their power which ultimately cost them dearly. [This excerpt found in the records of Captain Edward J. McClernand, Second Cavalry, (1866-'91)]

The Modoc Indians were a small tribe living in northern California near Tule Lake and Lost River. Through the intercession of interested civilians orders were issued for their removal to the Klamath Indian Reservation. They went on the reservation, but, on account of ill treatment left it, and the War Department was then directed to carry out the orders. The Indians at once commenced hostilities and one of the most protracted and obstinate Indian wars of later years followed.

Company B left Fort Klamath, Ore., November 28, 1872, for the purpose of arresting "Captain Jack" and the leaders of his band of Modocs, and at daylight on the 29th surprised the Indians in their camp near Lost River, Ore. They refused to surrender and an engagement followed in which 8 Indians were killed and many wounded, and the camp, squaws, and property were captured. The company lost 2 men killed and 6 wounded, 2 of them mortally. The company then went into camp at Crowley's Ranch on Lost River opposite the Indian camp.

Source: Quotes taken from Capt. Wainwright's "History of the 1st U.S. Cavalry," pp 156-180. Found at http://www.army.mil/cmh-pg/books/R&H/R&H-1CV.htm

Vocabulary:
chastisement = severe
    criticism or punishment
obstinate = stubborn
protracted = prolonged

War Department Plans

Discovery of gold in the Black Hills in 1874...and the extension of railroads into the area renewed unrest among the Indians, and many left their reservations. When the Indians would not comply with orders from the Interior Department to return to the reservations by the end of January 1876, the Army was requested to take action.

A small expedition into the Powder River country in March 1876 produced negligible results. Thereafter, a much larger operation, based on a War Department plan, was carried out in the early Summer months. As implemented by Lt. Gen. Philip Sheridan, commander of the Division of the Missouri (which included the Departments of the Missouri, Platte, and Dakota), the plan was to converge several columns simultaneously on the Yellowstone River where the Indians would be trapped and then forced to return to their reservations.

Vocabulary:

converge = to approach the same point from different directions

implemented = provided with a plan of action

negligible = not worth considering, trifling

Little Big Horn

The 7th Cavalry, proceeding up the Rosebud, discovered an encampment of 4,000 to 5,000 Indians (an estimated 2,500 warriors) on the Little Big Horn on 25 June 1876. Custer immediately ordered an attack, dividing his forces so as to strike the camp from several directions. The surprised Indians quickly rallied and drove off Maj. Marcus A. Reno's detachment (Companies A, G, and M) which suffered severe losses. Reno was joined by Capt. Frederick W. Benteen's detachment (Companies D, H, and K) and the pack train (including Company B) and this combined force was able to withstand heavy attacks which were finally lifted when the Indians withdrew late the following day. Custer and a force of 211 men (Companies C, E, F, I, and L) were surrounded and completely destroyed. Terry and Gibbon did not reach the scene of Custer's last stand until the morning of 27 June. The 7th Cavalry's total losses in this action (including Custer's detachment) were: 12 officers, 247 enlisted men, 5 civilians, and 3 Indian scouts killed; 2 officers and 51 enlisted men wounded.

On the Little Big Horn, near where the fight with Custer took place. (Library of Congress)

After this disaster the Little Big Horn campaign continued until September 1877 with many additional Regular units seeing action.... By the summer of 1877 most of the Sioux were back on the reservations. Crazy Horse had come in and was killed resisting arrest at Fort Robinson (Nebraska) in September. Sitting Bull, with a small band of Sioux, escaped to Canada but surrendered at Fort Buford (Montana) in July 1881.

...Chief Joseph, of the Nez Perces, may properly be termed the Indian Xenophon. His long retreat in 1877 through Idaho and Montana, pursued as he was by various columns of troops, is worthy of record in the annals of war. General Howard followed him with great persistence, but in vain. Norwood with his troop (L), brought him to stand at Camas Prairie, but

continued on next page

Vocabulary:

Xenophon = A Greek general and writer who lived around 400 B. C. He is famous for describing the retreat of 10,000 Greeks. (During the expedition called the Anabasis) being greatly overmatched in numbers, and not receiving the support he expected, was unable to detain the Indian chief long enough for General Howard to come up. The Troop made a gallant fight and reflected much credit upon the regiment. Gen. Gibbon, with part of the 7th Infantry, dealt Joseph a staggering blow on the bloody field of the Big Hole, and General Sturgis, with some of the 7th Cavalry, fought him on the Yellowstone, but all in vain, for the Indian general continued his headlong flight, and had he not stopped to procure buffalo meat when the close proximity of the British line gave him a feeling of security, his retreat would have been crowned with success. This halt enabled Miles with three troops of the 7th Cavalry, several companies of his own regiment, and Troops F, G and H of the Second, to strike the Nez Perces on Sept. 30 near the Bear Paw Mountains, and, after a desperate fight followed by a siege lasting until Oct. 6, to capture the greater part of the tribe. Thus it was that twice in this memorable campaign the Second Cavalry was represented, and upon two far distant fields. In the latter engagement Lieut. Jerome, Troop H, was made a prisoner and held for 24 hours, at the end of which time he was exchanged for Chief Joseph.

. . . .

In May, 1885, Chief Joseph and his followers, who were sent to the Indian Territory after their capture, were permitted to return to Washington Territory not far from their former home. It fell to the lot of Lieut. Carleton, with Troop L, to escort these people to the district assigned them. It was this troop that fought these Indians so valiantly at Camas Prairie in the summer of 1877, and now, eight years later, we find

Detail from Battle of Little Big Horn *by Kicking Bear (Mato Wanartaka) c. 1898, Lakota (born c. 1846) Watercolor on muslin, 2 ft. 11 in. x 5 ft. 10 in. (frame included).* (Courtesy of the The Southwest Museum, Los Angeles)

it escorting them as a guard against their white neighbors who threatened them.

· ·

Shining through the storms of fifty-six winters, the smoke of one hundred and seventeen combats and the dust of countless weary marches, appears the glorious roster of those men of the Second Cavalry who have shed their blood or lost their lives in service; a grand aggregate of forty-eight commissioned officers, and seven hundred and eight enlisted men.

Source: Captain Edward J. McClernand, Second Cavalry. (1866-'91). Found at http://www.army.mil/cmh-pg/reference/iwcmp.htm

Consider this:
What do you think of the tribute to the men of the Second Cavalry who lost their lives during the 56 years of battling Indians in the West?

Vocabulary:
aggregate = sum

Indian Speeches:
Native Americans Saw Their World Disappear

Chief Red Cloud on Indian Rights

Red Cloud, chief of the largest tribe of the Teton Sioux Nation, achieved early fame as a warrior and yet was one of the most influential Indian leaders to urge peace with the U.S. government. In 1870, Red Cloud visited the East, at which time be gave the following speech at a reception in his honor at Cooper Union in New York on July 16. Though a persistent critic of the government and of its Indian agents, whom be charged with graft [extortion] and corruption, Red Cloud only opposed agitation for further wars that, he knew, would only result in losses for his people.

Things to do:

Look back at the Two Row Wampum and see how it is like Red Cloud's speech.

What are the differences between the races, as described by Red Cloud? Do you agree with them? Explain your answer.

MY BRETHREN AND MY FRIENDS who are here before me this day, God Almighty has made us all, and He is here to bless what I have to say to you today. The Good Spirit made us both. He gave you lands and He gave us lands; He gave us these lands; you came in here, and we respected you as brothers. God Almighty made you but made you all white and clothed you; when He made us He made us with red skins and poor; now you have come.

When you first came we were very many, and you were few; now you are many, and we are getting very few, and we are poor. You do not know who appears before you today to speak. I am a representative of the original American race, the first people of this continent. We are good and not bad. The reports that you hear concerning us are all on one side. We are always well-disposed to them. You are here told that we are traders and thieves, and it is not so. We have given you nearly all our lands, and if we had any more land to give we would be very glad to give it. We have nothing more.

We are driven into a very little land, and we want you now, as our dear friends, to help us with the government of the United States.

The Great Father made us poor and ignorant —made you rich and wise and more skillful in these things that we know nothing about. The Great Father, the Good Father in Heaven, made you all to eat tame food—made us to eat wild food—gives us the wild food. You ask anybody who has gone through our country to California; ask those who have settled there and in Utah, and you will find that we have treated them always well. You have children; we have children. You want to raise your children and make them happy and prosperous; we want to raise and make them happy and prosperous. We ask you to help us to do it.

At the mouth of the Horse Creek, in 1852, the Great Father made a treaty with us by which we agreed to let all that country open for fifty-five years for the transit of those who were going through. We kept this treaty; we never treated any man wrong;...we never committed any murder or depredation until afterward the troops were sent into that country, and the troops killed our people and ill-treated them, and thus war and trouble arose; but before the troops were sent there we were quiet and peaceable, and there was no disturbance. Since that time there have been various goods sent from time to time to us, the only ones that ever reached us, and then after they reached us (very soon after) the government took them away. You, as good men, ought to help us to these goods.

Colonel Fitzpatrick of the government said we must all go to farm, and some of the people

continued on next page

Consider this:
Why do you think Red Cloud keeps praising and complimenting the U.S. government?

Why does he then criticize the treatment of the Indians by the government?

45

went to Fort Laramie and were badly treated. I only want to do that which is peaceful, and the Great Fathers know it, and also the Great Father who made us both. I came to Washington to see the Great Father in order to have peace and in order to have peace continue. That is all we want, and that is the reason why we are here now.

In 1868 men came out and brought papers. We are ignorant and do not read papers, and they did not tell us right what was in these papers. We wanted them to take away their forts, leave our country, would not make war, and give our traders something. They said we had bound ourselves to trade on the Missouri, and we said, no, we did not want that. The interpreters deceived us. When I went to Washington I saw the Great Father. The Great Father showed me what the treaties were; he showed me all these points and showed me that the interpreters had deceived me and did not let me know what the right side of the treaty was. All I want is right and justice.... I represent the Sioux Nation; they will be governed by what I say and what I represent....

Look at me. I am poor and naked, but I am the Chief of the Nation. We do not want riches, we do not ask for riches, but we want our children properly trained and brought up. We look to you for your sympathy. Our riches will...do us no good; we cannot take away into the other world anything we have—we want to have love and peace.... We would like to know why commissioners are sent out there to do nothing but rob [us] and get the riches of this world away from us? I was brought up among the traders and those who came out there in those early times. I had a good time for they treated us nicely and well. They taught me how

46

to wear clothes and use tobacco, and to use fire-arms and ammunition, and all went on very well until the Great Father sent out another kind of men—men who drank whisky. He sent out whisky-men, men who drank and quarreled, men who were so bad that he could not keep them at home, and so he sent them out there. I have sent a great many words to the Great Father, but I don't know that they ever reach the Great Father...so I thought I would come and tell you myself

...I am going back to my home. I want to tell the people that we cannot trust his agents and superintendents. I don't want strange people that we know nothing about.... I am very glad that we have come here and found you and that we can understand one another. I don't want any more such men sent out there, who are so poor that when they come out there their first thoughts are how they can fill their own pockets.

...We want honest men, and we want you to help to keep us in the lands that belong to us so that we may not be a prey to those who are viciously disposed. I am going back home. I am very glad that you have listened to me, and I wish you good-bye....

Source: Found at http://www.nv.cc.va.us/home/nvsageh/Hist122/Part1/RedCloud.htm

Consider this:
What does Red Cloud want for his people?

Chief Joseph's Lament

Very little of the spoken eloquence of Native Americans has survived, for painfully obvious reasons. But one great speech has become part of the American language. It was given in 1877 by the man known to whites as Chief Joseph (or, in the tongue of his people, Hinmaton-Yalaklit). He was a chief in the tribe that French explorers had named Nez Percé—"pierced nose"—because of their practice of wearing nose ornaments. When Joseph tried to lead a group of about 600 of his people out of Idaho to Canada to avoid reservation life, the United States army pursued them for over a thousand miles. On the long march, Joseph ran when he could and fought when he had to. Finally, only about thirty miles from Canada, with winter coming on and with about half of his men already wounded, Joseph surrendered.

Consider this:

Describe Chief Joseph's attitude toward the long battles between the Indians and the White man.

"Tell General Howard I know his heart.… What he told me before I have in my heart. I am tired of fighting. The old men are all dead. It is the young men who say yes or no. Tohoohoolzote [Joseph's brother] who led the young men is dead. It is cold, and we have no blankets. The little children are freezing to death. My people, some of them, have run away to the hills, and have no blankets, no food; no one knows where they are—perhaps freezing to death. I want to have some time to look for my children, and see how many I can find. Maybe I shall find them among the dead. Hear me, my chiefs, I am tired; my heart is sick and sad. From where the sun now stands, I will fight no more forever."

Source: Found at http://www.nv.cc.va.us/home/nvsageh/hist122/part1/indians

Sitting Bull, Life on the Sioux Reservation

The difficulties of "assimilation" into white society were poignantly [distressingly] illustrated in 1883, when the Sioux leader Sitting Bull testified before a committee of the United States that was visiting the Sioux reservation. The Sioux, like other tribes forced to live under the Dawes Act, had become dependent on a dole of blankets, food, and other necessities. Here, Sitting Bull tells the committee how life had been after he had listened to the "Great Father" (the president) and "came in" to the reservation.

Whatever you wanted of me I have obeyed. The Great Father sent me word that whatever he had against me in the past had been forgiven and thrown aside, and I accepted his promises and came in. And he told me not to step aside from the white man's path, and I am doing my best to travel in that path. I sit here and look around me now, and I see my people starving. We want cattle to butcher. That is the way you live, and we want to live the same way. When the Great Father told me to live like his people, I told him to send me six teams of mules, because that is the way the white people make a living. I asked for a horse and buggy for my children; I was advised to follow the ways of the white man, and that is why I asked for those things.

Source: Found at http://www.nv.cc.va.us/home/nvsageh/ hist122/part1/indians

Consider this:

Have you noticed the recurring theme of distrust in the Native American documents? Why, do you think, the U.S. government broke so many of its promises to the Indians?

If our government had kept its promises to the Indians, how might the U.S. be different today? Explain.

Crazy Horse: "I Have Spoken"

Crazy Horse, the great Oglala Sioux leader and hero of the Battle of the Little Big Horn, never had his photograph taken, and was on his deathbed before his thoughts were ever recorded on paper. Bayoneted by a Sioux guard at Fort Robinson, Nebraska, in 1877, he is supposed to have said these final words to Agent Jesse M. Lee.

Consider this:

List Crazy Horse's complaints against the White man. Was he right or wrong?

Things to do:

The Native Americans had a sense of pride and honesty that was not so prevalent with the white man. Support or refute this statement, using quotes from the documents in this book to support your answer.

Source: Found at http://www. nv.cc.va.us/home/nvsageh/ hist122/part1/indians

My friend, I do not blame you for this. Had I listened to you this trouble would not have happened to me. I was not hostile to the white man. Sometimes my young men would attack the Indians who were their enemies and took their ponies. They did it in return.

We had buffalo for food, and their hides for clothing and our tipis. We preferred hunting to a life of idleness on the reservations, where we were driven against our will. At times we did not get enough to eat, and we were not allowed to leave the reservation to hunt.

We preferred our own way of living. We were no expense to the government then. All we wanted was peace and to be left alone. Soldiers were sent out in the winter, who destroyed our villages. Then "Long Hair" [Custer] came in the same way. They say we massacred him, but he would have done the same to us had we not defended ourselves and fought to the last. Our first impulse was to escape with our squaws and papooses, but we were so hemmed in that we had to fight.

After that I went up on Tongue River with a few of my people and lived in peace. But the government would not let me alone. Finally, I came back to the Red Cloud Agency.... I came here with the agent [Lee] to talk with Big White Chief, but was not given a chance. They tried to confine me, I tried to escape, and a soldier ran his bayonet into me.

I have spoken.

CRAZY HORSE, Oglala Sioux

The Battle of Wounded Knee

The last major conflict in the Indian Wars took place on December 29, 1890, on the banks of Wounded Knee Creek. U.S. troops of the 7th Cavalry killed between 150 and 370 Sioux men, women, and children. Thirty-one U.S. soldiers were killed in action, many of them from fire by their own troops.

In the late 1880s, the Sioux had begun practicing a religion taught by Wovoka, a Paiute prophet, who promised that performing the ritual ghost dance would result in the return of native lands, the rise of dead ancestors, the disappearance of the whites, and a future of eternal peace and prosperity. During the fall of 1890, the Ghost Dance spread through the Sioux villages of the Dakota reservations, revitalizing the Indians. Nearby white settlers, frightened by the rituals, called for federal intervention.

The U.S. Army believed Chief Sitting Bull, who encouraged the dances, to be the instigator of an impending rebellion, and he was arrested in December 1890. As he was being led away over the objections of his supporters, a gunfight erupted. Thirteen people, including Sitting Bull, were killed. His followers then fled, some to the camp of Chief Big Foot. The 7th Cavalry pursued the Sioux to an encampment near Wounded Knee Creek. On December 29, 1890, a shot was fired within the camp and the army began shooting. The rest, as they say, is history. [Source: "Massacre At Wounded Knee, 1890," EyeWitness – history through the eyes of those who lived it, www.ibiscom.com (1998)]

Wovoka's message

...When you get home you must make a dance [the Ghost Dance] to continue five days. Dance four successive nights, and the last night keep up the dance until the morning of the fifth day, when all must bathe in the river and then disperse to their homes. You must all do in the same way.

I, Jack Wilson, love you all, and my heart is full of gladness for the gifts you have brought me. When you get home I shall give you a good cloud [rain?] which will make you feel good.

continued on next page

Consider this:

Is Wovoka's message a call to war or a spiritual message?

Why were the white soldiers afraid of the Ghost Dances?

I give you a good spirit and give you all good paint. I want you to come again in three months, some from each tribe there

…When the time comes there will be no more sickness, and everyone will be young again.

Do not refuse to work for the whites and do not make any trouble with them until you leave them. When the earth shakes [at the coming of the new world] do not be afraid. It will not hurt you.

I want you to dance every six weeks. Make a feast at the dance and have food that everybody may eat. Then bathe in the water. That is all. You will receive good words again from me some time. Do not tell lies.

Source: James Mooney, The Ghost-dance Religion and the Sioux Outbreak of 1890, 14th Annual Report of the Bureau of American Ethnology, Part 2 (1896). Note: James Mooney, an ethnologist with the Bureau of American Ethnology, was sent to investigate the Ghost Dance movement in 1891. He was given a transcript of Wovoka's message.

In the weeks leading up to the battle at Wounded Knee, newspapers around the country reported on developments in the area. A series of newspaper accounts and letters on the subject follows.

Vocabulary:
prudence = discretion, caution and wisdom in the conduct of affairs

Philadelphia Telegraph, Nov. 1, 1890

"If the army had charge of the Indians, as common sense and common prudence demand, Sitting Bull would be shut up very shortly, but the Army has no authority until the murdering redskins have broken out, burned a dozen ranches, slaughtered a score of women and children…. The Army officers may be perfectly well informed of Sitting Bull's intrigues, but they can do nothing until he deliberately perfects his rascally plans and gets ready to start his young bucks on a raid…."

Telegram to Washington, D.C.,
Nov. 15, 1890

"Indians are dancing in the snow and are wild and crazy. I have fully informed you that the employees and the government property at this agency have no protection and are at the mercy of the Ghost Dancers.... We need protection and we need it now ... nothing [short] of 1000 troops will stop this dancing."

– Dr. Daniel F. Royer, Agent,
Pine Ridge Agency

New York Times, Nov. 28, 1890

"…Couriers who have just reported to Gen. Brooke say that the redskins are dancing in circles…and their village has been so changed that the lodges form a circle.… When the couriers were before Gen. Brooke, the latter asked the significance of the circling Indians. One of the couriers, who is a half-breed, smiled and said: "The Sioux never dance that dance except for one purpose, and that is for war.""

Letter to the Indian Office
from Sitting Bull

"I want to write a few lines to let you know something. I have had a meeting with my Indians today, and I am writing to tell you our thoughts. God made both the white race and the Red race, and gave them minds and hearts to both. Then the white race gained a high place over the Indians. However, today our Father is helping us Indians—that is what we believe. And so I think this way. I wish no one to come with guns or knives to interfere with my prayers. All we are doing is praying for life and to learn how to do good...."

continued on next page

continued on next page

Consider this:

Is fear often aroused in people when they don't understand someone else's religious beliefs? Explain.

How does Sitting Bull try to ease the minds of the government and of the press?

53

Vocabulary:

tack = a course of
action meant to
minimize opposition

When you visited my camp you gave me good words about our prayers, but then you took your good words back again. And so I will let you know something. I got to go to [Pine Ridge] Agency and know this Pray [take part in the dance]: so I let you know that…I want answer back soon."

– Sitting Bull

Lieut. Bull Head or Shave Head, Grand River, Dec.14,1890

"From reports brought my Scout "Hawk Man" I believe the time has arrived for the arrest of Sitting Bull and that it can be made by the Indian Police without much risk—therefore I want you to make the arrest before daylight tomorrow morning....

Yours Respectfully,
James McLaughlin, U.S. Ind. Agent

P.S. You must not let him escape under any circumstances."

Brigadier General L.W. Colby, Commander, The Nebraska National Guard

"There was an understanding between the officers of the Indian and military departments that it would be impossible to bring Sitting Bull to Standing Rock alive, and even if successfully captured, it would be difficult to tell what to do with him. It was therefore believed that there was a tack arrangement between the commanding officers and the Indian police, that the death of the famous old Medicine man was much preferred to his capture, and that the slightest attempt to rescue him should be the signal for his destruction."

Orders to Colonel James. W. Forsyth , Dec. 28,1890

"Disarm the Indians. Take every precaution to prevent their escape. If they choose to fight, destroy them."

– By command of General Nelson Miles

Carl Smith, Chicago Inter-Ocean, Jan. 7, 1891

"Big Foot lay in a sort of solitary dignity.... He was dressed in fairly good civilian clothing, his head being tied up in a scarf. He had under-wear of wool and his general appearance was that of a fairly prosperous personage. He was shot through and through, and if he ever knew what hurt him, appearances dissembled very much. A wandering photographer propped the old man up, and as he lay there defenseless his portrait was taken...."

Source: Report of the Commissioner of Indian Affairs for 1891, volume 1, pages 179-181. Extracts from report of council held by delegations of Sioux with Commissioner of Indian Affairs, at Washington, February 11, 1891.

Miniconjou Sioux Chief Big Foot

The Battle of Wounded Knee (Smithsonian Institution)

Vocabulary:
desist = stop
exhorted = urged;
   advised

Lakota Accounts of the Massacre at Wounded Knee

SPOTTED HORSE. This man shot an officer in the army; the first shot killed this officer. I was a voluntary scout at that encounter and I saw exactly what was done, and that was what I noticed; that the first shot killed an officer. As soon as this shot was fired the Indians immediately began drawing their knives, and they were exhorted from all sides to desist, but this was not obeyed. Consequently the firing began immediately on the part of the soldiers....

TURNING HAWK. All the men who were in a bunch were killed right there, and those who escaped that first fire got into the ravine, and as they went along up the ravine for a long distance they were pursued on both sides by the soldiers and shot down, as the dead bodies showed afterwards. The women were standing off at a different place from where the men were stationed, and when the firing began, those of the men who escaped the first onslaught went in one direction up the ravine, and then the women, who were bunched together at another place, went entirely in a different direction through an open field, and the women fared the same fate as the men who went up the deep ravine.

AMERICAN HORSE...Of course we all feel very sad about this affair. I stood very loyal to the government all through those troublesome days, and believing so much in the government and being so loyal to it, my disappointment was very strong, and I have come to Washington with a very great blame on my heart. Of course it would have been all right if only the men were killed; we would feel almost grateful for it. But the fact of the killing of the women, and more especially the killing of the young boys and girls who are to go to make up the future strength of the Indian people, is the saddest part of the whole affair and we feel it very sorely....

Source: Report of the Commissioner of Indian Affairs for 1891, volume 1, pages 179-181. Extracts from report of council held by delegations of Sioux with Commissioner of Indian Affairs, at Washington, February 11, 1891.

Black Elk, December 29, 1890

"I did not know then how much was ended. When I look back now from this high hill of my old age, I can still see the butchered women and children lying heaped and scattered along the crooked gulch as plain as when I saw them with eyes still young. And I can see that something else died there in the bloody mud, and was buried in the blizzard. A people's dream died there. It was a beautiful dream.... The nation's hoop is broken and scattered. There is no center any longer, and the sacred tree is dead."

Source: Found at http://www.pbs.org/weta/thewest

Research Activities/Things to Do

The following excerpts reflect the attitudes of four people important in the conflicts between European American settlers moving west and the American Indians who had traditionally lived there. Read them and answer the questions on the next page.

1. Andrew Jackson to John McKee, 1794
(Spelling and punctuation modernized.)

"I fear that their Peace Talks are only Delusions and in order to put us off our guard. Why treat with them? Does not experience teach us that Treaties answer no other purpose than opening an easy door for the Indians to pass [through to] butcher our citizens.... Congress [should act] justly and punish the barbarians for murdering her innocent citizens; has not our [citizens] been prosecuted for marching to their [town] and killing some of them?... [The] Indians appear very troublesome [on the] frontier. [Settlers are] Discouraged and breaking and [num]bers [of them] leaving the Territory and moving [to] Kentucky. This country is declining [fast] and unless Congress lends us a more am[ple] protection this country will have at length [to break] or seek a protection from some other sources than the present."

Source: John Spencer Bassett, *Correspondence of Andrew Jackson,* (Washington: Carnegie Institution, 1926, pp. 12-3.

2. *Thomas Jefferson on the policy of "civilization," 1803.*

"When they [American Indians] withdraw themselves to the culture of a small piece of land, they will perceive how useless to them are extensive forests and will be willing to pare them [pieces of land] off from time to time in exchange for necessities for their farms and families. Should any tribe be foolhardy enough to take up the hatchet at any time, the seizing of the whole country of that tribe and driving them across the Mississippi as the only condition of peace, would be an example to others and a furtherance of our final consolidation."

Source: Moses Dawson, *A Historical Narrative of the Civil and Military Service of Major General William Henry Harrison,* Cincinnati, 1824, p. 36.

3. In 1811 Tecumseh traveled through the Southeast, attempting to gain recruits for the Pan-Indian movement.
The following is an excerpt from his speech to the Cherokee.

"Everywhere our people have passed away, as the snow of the mountains melts in May. We no longer rule the forest. The game has gone like our hunting grounds. Even our lands are nearly all gone. Yes, my brothers, our campfires are few. Those that still burn we must draw together.

"Behold what the white man has done to our people! Gone are the Pequot, the Narraganset, the Powhatan, the Tuscarora and the Coree.... We can no longer trust the white man. We gave him our tobacco and our maize. What happened? Now there is hardly land for us to grow these holy plants.

"White men have built their castles where the Indians' hunting grounds once were, and now they are coming into your mountain glens. Soon there will be no place for the Cherokee to hunt the deer and the bear. The tomahawk of the Shawnee is ready. Will the Cherokee raise the tomahawk? Will the Cherokee join their brothers the Shawnee?"

Source: W.C. Allen, *The Annals of Haywood County,* Waynesville, N.C.: 1935, pp. 44-6.

4. Junaluska, Tochalee and Chuliwa were Cherokee chiefs.
These were their responses to Tecumseh, 1811.

Junaluska: "It has been years, many years, since the Cherokee have drawn the tomahawk. Our braves have forgotten how to use the scalping knife. We have learned with sorrow it is better not to war against our white brothers.

We know that they have come to stay. They are like leaves in forest, they are so many. We believe we can live in peace with them. No more do they molest our lands. Our crops grow in peace...."

Tochalee and Chuliwa: "After years of distress we found ourselves in the power of a generous nation....We have prospered and increased, with the knowledge and practice of agriculture and other useful arts. Our cattle fill the forests, while wild animals dis-appear. Our daughters clothe us from spinning wheels and looms. Our youth have acquired knowledge of letters and figures. All we want is tranquility."

Source: W.C. Allen, *The Annals of Haywood County,* Waynesville, N.C.: 1935, pp. 44-6.

Questions on the Readings

1. Why, according to General Jackson, did American Indians negotiate treaties?
2. Who are the "other sources" Jackson said settlers would turn to if the U.S. government did not help them fight Indians?
3. How did Thomas Jefferson think the policy of "civilization" would help European American settlement?
4. What events did Tecumseh refer to in order to get the Cherokee to join him? Why?
5. What method did Tecumseh advocate to stop European American expansion?
6. What reasons did the Creek chiefs give for not joining Tecumseh?
7. How did Jackson's and Tecumseh's view of the origins of European American/ American Indian conflict compare?

Source: http://www.cr.nps.gov/nr/twhp/wwwlps/lessons/54horseshoe/54facts2.htm

Suggested Further Reading

The books listed below are suggested readings in American literature, which tie in with *The Indian Wars: Researching American History Series*. The selections were made based on feedback from teachers and librarians currently using them in interdisciplinary classes for students in grades 4 to 12. Of course there are many other historical novels that would be appropriate to tie in with the titles in this series.

Cherokee Trail, Lewis L'Amour - HS

Moccasin Trail, Eloise Jarvis McGraw (Crow) - M

Bearstone, Will Hobbs - M

Sing Down the Moon, Scott O'Dell (Navajo) - M

Where the Broken Heart Still Beats: The Story of Cynthia Ann Parker, Carolyn Meyer (Comanche) - M

Light in the Forest, Conrad Richter - M

Save the Queen of Sheba, Louise Moeri - M

*Last of the Mohicans * Deerslayer * The Pathfinder * The Leatherstocking Tales,* James Fenimore Cooper - HS

Web Sites

http://www.geocities.com/Athens/Parthenon/150

http://www.militaryheritage.com

http://www.kidinfo.com/American_History

http://www.yourhistorylink.com/war/eighteenthcent

http://www.buffalosoldier.net

http://www.ajourneypast.com/researchmilitarys

http://tuscaroras.com

http://www.rootsweb.com/~nalakota

For information on these and other titles from Discovery Enterprises, Ltd., call or write to: Discovery Enterprises, Ltd., 31 Laurelwood Drive, Carlisle, MA 01741 Phone: 978-287-5401 Fax: 978-287-5402. Visit our website at www.ushistorydocs.com